Island
of
Dreams

Jasminne Mendez

Floricanto Press

Floricanto Press
7177 Walnut Canyon Rd.
Moorpark, California 93021
(415) 793-2662
www. floricantopress. com

ISBN-13: 978-1493580880

"Por nuestra cultura hablarán nuestros libros. Our books shall speak for our culture."

Roberto Cabello-Argandoña, Editor

"Disorder" was first published in *Magnolia: A Journal of Women's Socially Engaged Literature* Volume II © June 2012.

Author's photo by Sayra Contreras

Para mis padres, Sonia y Benjamín

For my parents

*"I may not have gone where I intended to go, but I think
I am where I was intended to be."*

-Douglas Adams

Acknowledgements

I am truly blessed. I know this because not only have I been given the time, the space, and the support I needed to complete this book, but because I have also been showered with love in the process. This memoir never would have been possible without the guidance, energy and laughter of my husband Lupe Mendez. He believed in me despite my pessimism, held my hand when I wanted to let go, and gave me a room of my own when I needed it most. Eight years ago, I walked into a poetry reading hoping he'd ask me out on a date, and now, some of those same poems have made it into this book because of him. Thank you, for never allowing me to close the door on myself and become an island.

I would also like to thank my parents, Sonia and Benjamin for bringing me into this world and never giving up on me. Gracias por creer en mí y por siempre estar a mi lado. Los quiero mucho. A big hug and lots of love goes out to my sister, Jenny who always listened and never failed to give her honest opinion just to keep things real for all of us. Thank you to my brother, Ben, for introducing me to the wonderful world of literature and the arts. It is because of you that I realized how art could change and save my life.

Thank you to my tías, abuelas, and primas for being the best role models a young Latina could ask for. Without you, this book and my life would lack humor, compassion, and good food. Las quiero mucho a todas. To the young ladies at Cristo Rey Jesuit, Alexis, Xochytl, and Ebony and my friends

Hana, Ivy, and Alicia who read the book in its early stages and gave honest and thoughtful feedback.

It is also with the help, support, and advice of a select group of mentors, organizations and special individuals that this book is possible. A great debt of gratitude goes to my mentor and friend, Sarah Cortez, for always encouraging me to pursue writing and for guiding me through the revision and editing process. Thank you to the Houston writer's group Nuestra Palabra and Tony Diaz for believing in me and providing me with generous opportunities to share my work over the last eight years. Without your platform and support, I'd still be reading poetry out of a tattered journal in a dimly lit coffee house. Lastly, thank you to my publisher, Floricanto Press for seeing the potential in this work and for your willingness to bring it to fruition. You took a chance on me, and I am forever grateful.

Finally, I would like to thank *Baby M*. Though I never met you, your brief presence gave me the strength, courage, and wisdom to pursue my dreams. You helped me understand that life is precious, our time here on Earth is short, and that the things that are worth having are worth fighting for. We will meet again one day.

Island of Dreams

Contents

Common Ground

It is solved by walking. As I walk, I remember, and as I remember I try to understand how the story of my life is woven together. There are no seams, no buttons or snaps to hold it all in place. There are only fragmented moments of powerful emotions, gentle laughter, and quiet tears between bed sheets. A single song and road trips with the *familia* bake in the oven of my childhood like a soft vanilla cake, warm and sweet. The memories begin to melt in my mouth and I inhale the stories remembering and understanding it all as I walk.

§ § §

Clumsily and loudly I sang: "And I said what about Breakfast at Tiffany's, she said, 'I think, I remember the film and . . . !'"

"Shut up!" my sister screamed at me.

"You shut up," I retorted, "I'm only singing. Leave me alone." I tossed a pillow at her hoping to inflict pain.

"But I want to hear the SONG, not YOU!" She rolled her eyes and sank into her seat.

"Yamina! *Déjala,*" my brother interjected, trying to be the peacekeeper.

"I didn't even do anything to her! She's the one getting all annoyed."

"Dude, she's just a kid. You know better."

"Man, whatever. I'll sing if I want to."

"Yamina!" My brother was fed up.

"Hey, *qué pasa*" my mom interrupted. She looked in the rear-view mirror, her stern face scolding us, her free hand wailing wildly and ready to pinch whoever was near.

"NADA!" we yelled. We knew that if any of us complained, all three of us would pay the price. Only four hours into our road trip, and we already couldn't stand each other. This, however, was nothing new. For the next twenty-one hours, we would fight over the radio, the blankets, the front seat, the ice cooler, and the camera. My sister would sprawl herself all over the back seat of the van, while my brother and I would stretch our legs and crick our necks in the two single seats between the back seat and the driver's seat. Uncomfortable, hungry, impatient and bored we would push each other's buttons for a laugh, and make fun of *Papi* who would always push the brakes harder than necessary and drive either too slow or not fast enough.

Mami had taken the wheel to let *Papi* rest for a while, but that always backfired because he could never trust my mom long enough to fall asleep. He would close his eyes for a few minutes at a time then quickly adjust himself and grunt: "we'll be there at thirteen-hundred hours" like a narcoleptic soldier waiting for war.

The yelling and my mom's threat woke *Papi* up, "*Qué te dije mujer*, focus on the road and leave the kids alone. *Tenemos que llegar* by zero-eight-hundred hours tomorrow morning."

"*Yo sé, pero* these kids are driving me crazy!" *Mami* was frustrated that she had had to put up with us and with my father's constant nagging. She was tired of the fighting, scared about the rain that had begun pouring down on the narrow freeway, and upset because *Papi* had refused to bring Mama, her mother, with us.

"Just pay attention to the road, and watch your speed limit. It says 55 but it's raining, so slow down," my father said calmly. He readjusted his hat, crossed his arms, closed his eyes, and told my mother to let him know when she wanted him to take the wheel again.

"*Ay Pa*, just go back to sleep and let *Mami* drive," I said. My father turned around and looked at me. Stubborn, impatient and bold, I was, no doubt, my father's daughter.

"*Déjame tranquilo,* ok," he warned. I sank down into my seat and wondered: are we there yet?

We were on our annual road trip. This year we were driving from small town Clarksville, Tennessee to see our aunts and cousins on my dad's side in Brooklyn, New York. We were all excited to be able to go back to New York. We missed our cousins and knew that our aunts would shower us with welcome gifts and unwelcome criticism. My aunts, while generally well intentioned, never failed to make us all feel horrible about ourselves regardless of how much effort we put into our hair, our clothes, our diet, or our gifts.

"Oh, *mira* how nice. It's for the kitchen, no? Well I already have two of these, *pero* it's nice," one would say, referring to a gift my mother had desperately hand-picked and mulled over for weeks.

"*Mira, niña* you're getting *gordita,* look at all these little love handles, and your cheeks, eating too much rice, *no crees*?" Another aunt would chime in.

"Those jeans didn't come in any other size? They seem a bit small; you should give them to your cousin Miguel. They'd look better on him."

Hard criticism that I had learned to ignore, smile through, and write evil come backs for in my journals on the trip back home. My sister, on the other hand, had not learned to ignore the comments. She was offended by them and took them personally. She would smack her teeth and let everyone know: "I look fine. Leave me alone, and if I go on a diet maybe you should join me."

My mother would hiss at her, "Jenny! Don't be disrespectful." My aunts would laugh, and proceed to offer her a plate of food for those growing bones and muscles.

Ben, my brother always managed to stay out of every conversation. He would briefly nod his head, give a half-fake smile to everyone in the room, hug them like they were all lepers, and go sit on the couch to play video games or watch TV. I hated his ability to do that, and still do. My sister and I always had to stay in the kitchen, helping everyone else cook and clean, to prove that my mother had raised us right, while all the boys and men got to sit and watch TV. We did the hard work while they waited for the dinner table to be set.

That morning, in the car, I was unaware that those moments would shape my future actions. I was more excited about the snow, and the gifts, and all the girl talk I would stay up all night having with my cousins. The song ended, and in an effort to stop the bickering, *Mami* had put in an Ana Gabriel tape into the tape player. We moaned and smacked our teeth.

"We hate this music. We'll stop arguing, I promise." Although I secretly enjoyed this old people music, I didn't want my siblings to know this. Besides, I really was enjoying listening to music in English for once. But *Mami* rejected my complaint and said, "*No me importa*. I'm driving, I get to listen to what I want to now."

Fine, I thought, and wrapped myself up in my blanket, fluffed my pillow, and fell asleep for as long as I could to make the ride bearable. While I slept, I find out later, we stopped for gas, snacks, and because Jenny wasn't feeling well. Apparently, the pizza we had eaten for lunch had made her sick. She had thrown up all over the parking lot of the gas station and had to change her shirt and shoes. I woke up when my dad turned the van on and because Ben was yelling, "Ew, that was so gross!"

"Leave me alone," Jenny yelled from the back. "I don't feel good. Stop making fun of me."

"What the hell is going on?" I asked.

"Dude, you missed it, Jenny threw up everywhere."

"What?! Where everywhere?" I sat up quickly looking around the van for signs of mushy pizza slices and stomach acid.

"Well, not in here, but in the freaking parking lot at the gas station."

"Aw man, that's gross." I turned in my seat, away from her.

"Shut up, already! I know it's gross." Jenny shoved her head in a pillow, and curled up in a fetal position.

"Sorry, Jen. Are you feeling better?"

"No."

"*Ya*, leave her alone," *Mami* said. "The both of you either go to sleep, or read a book, but leave her alone." My mom was now in the passenger's seat and had had enough of the trip since my sister's fiasco. "We have fifteen hours to go, and we're not stopping unless it's an emergency, so relax and stop fighting."

"I can't read in the car; I get car sick," I whined.

"Mina, shut up and go back to sleep." My brother went back to playing his video game and was yet again trying to keep the peace. It was, after all, his only job in the family.

"Pa, can you put the radio on?" I give him my best, sweet

"daddy's little girl" voice and he conceded. The stations had all changed, and the one from home was long gone. I unbuckled my seat belt and wedged myself between the driver's seat and the passenger's seat. I began to play with the radio trying to find a good station I could listen to for at least an hour.

"Hurry up, Yamina, and sit back down. You shouldn't be up without your seat belt on." *Mami* was always worrying, and that always annoyed me.

"Hold on."

"*Si nos para la policía,*" *Mami* warned, "you'll see what I'll be 'holding on' to!" *Mami* hated being stopped by the police. She said it was embarrassing and she worried about *el qué dirán*. I don't know who she though would say anything or criticize us for being stopped by the police since no one would have known if we didn't tell them.

"Ok, ok, *ya*." I had found a local top forties station that was slowly fading, but that would have to do for the time being. I went back to my seat and stared out the window. The landscape was a sea of grassless hills, barren trees, and muddy swamps. There was nothing to see. I began to count cars and read billboards. The advertisements for KFC and Burger King made me hungry.

"When are we going to stop for dinner?" I asked. I knew that the topic of food would make us come together and feel happy again.

"Around seven. Eat some chips or have a sandwich from the cooler until then." My mom reached around, opened the ice cooler and handed me a cheese and turkey sandwich.

"*Gracias,*" I said. I took a bite of a cold soggy sandwich and opened a bag of chips.

"Want some juice?"

"*Sí*, please." My mom handed me a juice box and reached into her purse for a brush.

"Here, take this too. *Péinate.*" Our temporary peace treaty, created by the mention of food, was broken with that simple gesture.

"Ma! I don't need a brush. I'm in a car and no one is going to see me. I'll comb it before I get out."

"¡*Está bien!* She cursed, turned around, pulled her visor down and used the brush to smooth out the frizz in her own hair instead. Back to being enemies, I thought. Oh well, it was easier this way. The less we talked, the less there was to get upset about.

In an effort to calm the storm that had begun inside our car, my father turned the radio down and in broken English said, "You wan to hear a *yoke*?" He raised his eyebrows and peeked into the rearview mirror. He smiled, knowing we couldn't deny him this one simple pleasure. After twelve years in the Army, my father had a pantry full of stale "yokes" and useless riddles. The three of us groaned a barely audible "ok" and he began.

"A Russian, an African and a Mexican go in to take the last part of their U.S. citizenship test," he paused, waited for a chuckle, and continued, "the Russian walks into the office . . . " I began to fade him out. I'd heard this joke before. I didn't want to spoil his fun, so I stared out the window instead. I began to daydream about growing up.

In my fantasy I was not dressed all in white, heading to the altar. Instead, I saw myself on a Broadway stage, winning a Tony award. I heard the announcer say, "This is her first Tony award and she is the first Latina to ever receive such a nomination." I had big, inconceivable dreams then, but I let myself dream them, even if only sometimes. I smiled, my face pressed against the car window, fogging up the glass, until my brother pushed me.

"You thought that was funny?"

"What? No! I wasn't even listening to him."

"Oh," he said, and continued pushing the buttons on his videogame consul.

I sighed and tried to fade out the old school *bachata* remix in the background so I could return to my pleasant ponderings. The dreams about my future always involved New York, or acting, or, at least just getting out of my parent's house. I wanted desperately to escape my father's judgmental eye and my mother's nagging. I knew very early on that it would be almost impossible to live up to my father's expectations and quite near a miracle if I were ever to become the perfect homemaker my mother wanted me to be. So instead, I pleased them sometimes, rebelled often, and made plans for leaving home as soon as possible. My usual fantasies of becoming famous sent me into a quiet slumber. As my cheek pressed against the window, the seat belt stroked my neck, and a quiet merengue played on the radio lulling me back to sleep.

I must have slept for at least five hours because when I woke up it was dark outside and my father said we were stopping for dinner. On our family road trips, there were only two types of food my father agreed to spend money on: pizza or a buffet. We were now parked in front of a Ryan's Steakhouse Buffet. In those days we lived and died for Ryan's. It was the only time we could escape the drudgery of rice and beans and fried plantains. That night, as always, we gorged ourselves on mashed potatoes, fried chicken, spaghetti, and macaroni and cheese. We were in food paradise, and eventually, back in the car and in a food coma.

The rest of the drive up was pretty uneventful. We slept. We argued. We stopped to pee at questionable, unsanitary gas-station bathrooms. We laughed and complained about *Papi*'s driving. Then, several Virginias, a turnpike and a tunnel, and one Brooklyn Bridge later we were finally at my aunt's house. Like a basket of dirty laundry going into the wash, we unloaded our bags and our bodies onto the doorstep. Everyone was there to greet us. A scattered collage of noise began.

"Yamina!"

"Jenny!"

"¡Benjamín y Sonia! ¡Qué gusto!"

There were hugs and kisses.

"Look at you Ben! So tall already!"

"What's wrong guys? You tired?"

"You hungry?"

There were plates of food. And more food. It was awful. And yet, it was awesome. Despite the fatigue of being in a car for two days and the fact that we knew we would sleep on someone's floor for the next four, we knew were surrounded by love.

It was this love that showed its true strength the next day on Christmas Eve. Mid-afternoon, when the *pernil* was roasting and the beans were boiling, my father got a foreboding call from my uncle. My *Tío* Nando was supposed to be housesitting while we were away. He apparently had failed. The morning of Christmas Eve, my uncle called my aunt's house in New York and asked *Papi* if we had taken the Nintendo player with us. My father said no. My uncle proceeded to ask the same question about a variety of valuable items. The VCR? The stereo? Finally, my father, in his usual impatient manner lashed out, "What is this all about? Why are you asking me this?"

"I think someone broke into the house. All of those things are missing."

We'd been robbed.

"How did this happen?" My father was furious. I could also tell that my uncle's ineptitude was pushing him to his limit.

"I don't know," *Tío* Nando said. "I went out last night and when I came back everything seemed normal. But when I looked around this morning there were things out of place."

This conversation went on for about another two minutes and got progressively worse. My father paced the room. My mother started to wipe down countertops. I had been watching TV during the whole conversation and when I was able to make sense of what was happening, I ran to my cousin's bedroom.

"Ben, Jenny, I think we've been robbed!" I whispered loudly.

"What? Here? Did someone break in?" my sister asked.

"No, dummy, at the house, our house. Back home."

"What!? What did they take? How do you know?" My brother looked frantically back and forth from his video game to me and back to his video game so as not to "die."

"Dad's on the phone with *Tío*. Come on, we gotta find out." I grabbed my sister by the arm and dragged her to the kitchen.

I was what you call, *entremetía*, or nosy. I loved gossip and drama then as much as I do now, especially family adult drama. My sister followed me into the kitchen close behind. I pulled up close to *Mami*'s shoulder and whispered: "*¿Qué pasó?*" I knew not to ask *Papi*, because he would just get angry or blow me off. I asked her again what had happened.

"Someone broke into the house. They took some things. Here, put these plates up and go wash your hair." I knew that this was all I was going to squeeze out of her at that moment. She was too frazzled and was trying to cope. Her house, the home she had built and kept with bleach, baked goods, and elbow grease had been desecrated, and there was nothing she could do to fix it. She was twenty-three hours away, in someone else's home, scrubbing someone else's pots and pans. Her only option, to calm her nerves, was to keep cooking and cleaning.

"Fine," I mumbled and did as I was told. I knew the situation was too sensitive and too new to bother fighting with her. My incesssnt curiosity would only have made matters worse.

Later that night, before Christmas Eve dinner, *Papi* took the whole family aside into my Grandmother's bedroom. Ben, Jenny and I sat on the edge of the bed and my mother leaned on the dresser. Very sternly, my father began, "Last night someone broke into the house and stole some things. We were robbed. No one was hurt. But I don't want you to worry about that right now. The house is fine. We are fine and we are going to enjoy our Christmas. We don't need to talk about it anymore. This is not going to ruin our time *con la familia.* Do you understand?" He crossed his arms definitively and peered at us over his glasses.

When my father spoke, it was always an order. We had been commanded to enjoy Christmas and "understand." We all nodded our heads. *Mami* gathered us all for a hug.

"*Gracias a Dios,* we are all here. We are all safe. That's what matters." She fought back tears. I hugged her tightly. It seemed like my parent's fifteen-years-in-the-making

American dream had been shattered. Their safety and livelihood had been threatened and their hands were tied. I started to choke up, but *Mami* looked at me and said, "*No, no llores.* It's Christmas and we are all together as a family, and you still have gifts to open. There is nothing to be sad about." I knew she was right. We left the bedroom and went to the dining room table to begin Christmas Eve dinner.

That night, we enjoyed *pernil*, rice and beans, fried plantains, potato salad, and *flan*. At midnight, as was the tradition in my family, we opened gifts. The stuff we had lost had been replaced by new stuff. We ran around the room, drowning in wrapping paper, and showing off our new gizmos, gadgets, and games. We enjoyed our Christmas just like *Papi* ordered.

§ § §

As I walk to my car, carrying boxes of stuff, on the day before I leave to college, I remember that road trip and all the others like it. I am suddenly filled with sadness and longing for those simpler times because I realize that this is one road trip I will have to take alone. It is the beginning of my American dream and the culmination of my parents'. And yet, the memories of the "Christmas we were robbed" and all the others like it stew in the crockpot of my mind and the smell and taste of family, togetherness, love, and tradition remind me that I didn't achieve all of this on my own. I know now that *Mami* and *Papi*'s dreams fueled mine. My family has helped make me who I am and who I'm going to be. I realize now, that in order to move forward we have to understand and appreciate where we've been.

Disorder

I have a disorder:
Dissociative Identity Disorder
formerly known as
Multiple Personality Disorder,
in my case, is known as
Multiple Dissociative Personality Identity Cultural
Disorder.

The terms and conditions of my disorder
cause me to border
on insanity and
abnormality.

Condition I

I am, *yo soy,*
Dominicana, Dominican.
You can call me Latina, Hispanic,
Caribbean or just strange.
I like fried plantains,
Arroz con pollo,
And Juan Luis Guerra playing on through the night.
I like to dance, sing,

And understand that unless I'm in my own country
I will be labeled black, mixed, Puerto Rican, spic.
Everything but what I really am,
A Dominican.

Condition II

Left, right, left, right, left
I am a military brat.
Yes, Father, *Padre mío*, I promise to do everything
to serve and protect
my country.
I am from here and there and everywhere
all at once.
I lack stability and
Crave mobility.
Constantly changing,
Constantly moving, constantly leaving and losing
friends.

Condition III

I'm black and I'm proud.
But what I lack,
is a shroud
of dignity
to stand up and destroy your ability

to categorize me
into another statistical minority.
If I were black, I would be proud.
But I'm not,
so I'm just offended.

Condition IV

I am an American.
I eat McDonalds.
I drink Coca-Cola®.
I went to prom.
I lost my virginity at 16.
I drive a foreign car.
I go to college.
And I want a white picket fence, with a minivan
and 2.3 children
and yes, a husband who will eventually leave me
for another man.
Welcome to the American Dream.

Condition V

I am a Catholic.
En el nombre del Padre, del hijo, y del espíritu santo.

I believe in one holy, Catholic, and Apostolic church.

I believe in abortion, birth-control, gay marriage, God, Jesus

and reincarnation.

I acknowledge one baptism for the forgiveness of sins,

and I acknowledge that no one is perfect, and I accept

everyone for who they are and what they believe

gay, straight, bi, tri, trans, man woman and child.

But lead me not into temptation, and I will follow

all ten commandments.

In the name of the Father, the Son and

the Holy Spirit.

Amen.

Condition VI

I am still a child,

wanting to be a woman,

and only growing up to be confused.

I want to play with Barbie and Ken,

but now Barbie has lost her head,

and so have I.

I will always be a girl,

but I was not always a woman.

Condition VII

I am a student, a teacher,

a learner, and a giver.

I am what most people are afraid to be.

I am someone who is okay with having more than

one identity.

I hope and yearn for things to be.

I love and accept those around me.

If I cannot tell you distinctly where I am from, it is because

I am everyone and from everywhere.

I am that and much, much, much,

much, much, much more.

Condition VIII

I am, *yo soy, la reflexión de mi madre.*

I am, *yo soy,* a reflection of my mother.

First Love

Tío Luis was my first love, but after he was deported, I never saw him again. I didn't want to resent him for leaving me, so I made up stories about what could have happened to him. By the time I was twelve, however, I realized I *never* would see him again, and I convinced myself he'd been sent to Guantanamo Bay.

He came to the house only twice. Once when I was four, and again when I was five. He stood at the door, the tallest man I'd ever seen, holding a brown suitcase that had obviously traveled too far. A bearded gentleman, with dark hair and soft but tired eyes, hugged my mom. I reached for her hip, and ran into his calf. He looked down at me and smiled, his teeth too big for his mouth.

"Sonia!" he said to my mother, and the vibration of his voice ran down his body and into mine. "This must be Yamina," and he dropped his suitcase like a man who'd already been carrying too much baggage. His knees, which ached from years of hard labor, bent slowly until his face reached mine. I continued to clutch my mom's dress. "*Qué linda,*" he said sincerely and pinched my cheeks.

I let go of my mother and hugged this complete stranger simply because he had called me beautiful and meant it. He picked me up with a gentle grunt, and laughed the way the earth quakes, and my whole body shook. I buried my head in the pillow of his neck and shoulder and breathed him in. He smelled raw. He smelled sweet. Fresh salt water leaked from his pores and nicotine coated in peppermint floated from his lips.

At age four, I had developed my first crush. I was destined to fall in love with this man. Nestled in his arms, I felt safe. I felt quiet. I felt real. Finally, a man that didn't yell and thought I was beautiful. I wanted him to stay.

My mom took his suitcase and the three of us went inside. He sat me down on the couch, carefully, like a well-earned trophy being placed on a mantle. I sat as close to him as I could, and he put his arms around me. I felt warm. I looked over at my mom and she was smiling. It was a smile that stretched from the inside of our quiet home all the way out to the tumultuous past my mom was now facing. I knew that this man was important, and his presence meant something.

My mother leaned forward and squeezed his knees. "*Hermano*," she said. I giggled, and broke the tender moment between brother and sister because I finally understood who he was.

"It's been too long," he said regretfully.

"I know, I know," replied *Mami*. "*Mija*," she said, looking at me with pride in her eyes, "This is your *Tío* Luis. Ask him for your blessing." I quickly readjusted myself to look him straight in the eye, and I said, "*Bendición, Tío.*"

And he dutifully replied, "God bless you, Yamina." He moved the hair out of my eyes, and I giggled again. Yes, I was in love.

"Well, now that you're here, what would you like to eat? It was a long flight, you must be starving."

"*Hermana,* what do you think I want?"

"Your favorite?"

"Only if it's not too much trouble."

"Meatballs and white rice, *a sus órdenes.*" *Mami* paused, and said, "That is still your favorite, right?"

"Why of course. Some things don't ever change, Sonia." He chuckled, as if trying to push back the knot in his throat, and my mom hugged him again. I hugged him again too, but not really understanding why. They both laughed at my gesture and we all walked into the kitchen to watch my mom cook dinner.

That night we ate ground beef meatballs with white rice. *Mami* had never made this meal before, and I wonder now if it was because it brought back too many memories. At dinner we licked our sauce-covered fingers and listened to my uncle's stories about life in New York, the children he'd lost track of, and the motorcycle back in the Dominican Republic that he missed more than his own family. His first visit seemed pleasant. It was unexpected, but pleasant. He stayed for four days and helped my mom with chores during the day. He played with my dolls and me. I became infatuated. He laughed with me. He hugged me. He still called me beautiful. This man was not my father. This man was tender. I wanted him to stay.

A year later, when he visited again, he came with a blue duffle bag and arrived in the middle of the night. I heard whispers from my bedroom, my mother crying, and his giant voice repeating over and over *"Yo no se, yo no se, Sonia."* For three days, my parents and *Tío* Luis sat around the dining room table drowning in a sea of papers and phone calls. No one ate meatballs this time. My mom barely even cooked, which was unusual, and I sat in my room alone, playing with dolls and trying to figure out what it was my uncle "didn't know."

On the third day of his visit, he sat on the living room couch tired and defeated. I went over to him and put my head down on his lap. He stroked my hair gently until I fell asleep feeling safe, warm, quiet and real.

When I woke up, he was gone. My mother was in the kitchen about to cook dinner. I went to her and asked if she was going to cook meatballs with white rice for my uncle.

"No," she said, "your father took *Tío* Luis to the airport. He had to go." She lit the gas stove with a match and told me to pass her the salt.

Plátanos & Potatoes

Plátanos:
In the DR you can:
Bake/Broil/Boil
Fry/Beat
Smash/Mash
Roll
Deep fry/Re-fry
Twice bake/Re-bake
Sweeten/Solidify
Or even
Sauté
A plantain

Potatoes:

In America you can:
Sauté/Solidify/Sweeten
Re-bake/Twice bake
Re-fry/Deep fry
Roll
Mash/Smash
Beat/Fry
Boil/Broil/
Or even

Bake

A potato

Growing up, *Mami* only cooks plantains.

But I really like *papas*.

Mami says that's not "food."

Every day in high school, I eat a baked potato.

When I go away to college,

I will only eat potatoes.

I will not know how to buy plantains,

Always wondering are they *verdes* o *maduros*?

Mami will come to town and buy them for me.

They will spoil in my empty fridge.

The Apple & The Tree

Periwinkle purple and yellow were the colors for my *Quinceañera*. Well, it should have been a *Quinceañera*, but it was actually a sweet sixteen. *Mami* and *Papi* didn't have the money when I turned 15 so I had to wait a year to get the party of my dreams. Yep, everything was purple. From the flower arrangements to the table settings and my nail polish, everything was purple. The theme of the event was angels. From the age of nine to seventeen I was obsessed with collecting porcelain angel knick-knacks, so it was only fitting that my rite of passage party be adorned with angel figurines. Porcelain angel vases lined with purple and yellow plastic pearls decorated every table. I even insisted that the extravagant three-tier birthday cake I had a family friend slave over, be covered in angelic adornments.

My mom, sister, and four *tías* spent hours upon hours hot gluing beads, lace and silk flowers onto everything I wanted for my coming of age day. I, on the other hand, spent most of the time barking orders and whining my way into getting what I wanted, or in those days thought that I *needed,* from my father. A catered American dinner to start, no *plátanos fritos* or rice and beans for my friends because I knew their taste buds would not understand the complexities of a traditional Dominican dish. Next, I swooned over a large and elegant dress that would later hang in my closet turning the same color yellow the embroidered invitations I begged for were made in. A DJ, tiara, diamond earrings and a pre-day photo shoot completed the birthday package I knew I had earned. I wanted these things because I wanted everything to be perfect. I wanted everyone to have fun and remember my party. And it did turn out to be a great party. Many memories were made and many lifetime friendships solidified. But there are some moments of the party planning process that I regret. Moments that hurt the very people who were only trying to give me everything I wanted.

This part of the story hurts. I find it difficult to think about and even harder to admit. A child should never make their mother or father cry unless it is out of joy. I am ashamed now, as I remember, of that horrible moment when my mother's unconditional love for me turned into disappointment and sadness. One moment of a few unfiltered words coming from my teenage angst mouth were enough to create a stain on the relationship between my mother and me forever.

It was two weeks before the party and we stood in line at the cash register of the Sally Beauty Supply store. I had picked out the perfect shade of periwinkle purple nail polish, eye shadow and hair accessories. My mom had two boxes of hair dye in her hands and needed help figuring out which one would last longer and not fade. She wanted a new look for the party and wanted the color to last. Her ability to read, write and speak English, at the time, was not what it is now; so, she asked me read the boxes and figure it out. I was testing the purple polish on my nails and became very agitated that she had interrupted this delicate process. I stopped what I was doing, glanced at the two boxes and shrugged, "I don't know."

"*Cómo que,* 'you don't know,' *léelo,* read it!"

"¡Ma, I told you, *yo no sé!*"

"*Pues,* ask *la cajera.*" She plopped the two boxes down on the counter, stared at me and then at the cashier. "¡*Pregúntale!*" she ordered.

I sighed again and said, "I don't know what you want me to ask her!" I had forgotten her original question because my mind had drifted to thinking about the crush I had invited, and in my mind, as the nail polish dried and my mother steamed, I saw us dancing and laughing the night away. The lady at the cash register interrupted our spat.

"Can I help you?" she asked.

"Jes, which won?" asked my mom in her broken English, frustration and embarrassment rising in her voice and collecting in her eyes.

"Um, which one what?"

"Gwich won?" *Mami* repeated, holding up both boxes next to her hair.

"Ma'am, I don't know what you're asking. Sweetie, what does your mom need?"

Aloof and upset, I finally looked up from my partially painted nails, stared at my mom, and then at the cashier.

"Um, I don't know," I said. I looked at *Mami* and asked

her, "*¿Qué es lo que quieres Ma?* I don't know what you want." My mother stood wide-eyed, shaking and ravenous like a lioness ready for the hunt.

"*¡¿Cuál dura más!?*" She yelled. She wanted to know which hair dye would last the longest. "*¡Pregúntale!*" Her voice finally cracked after trying to keep it together through fractured sentences of a language that had suddenly stolen her pride.

"*Ay*, gosh Mom, it's not that hard. Look, it says permanent on one and semi-permanent on the other, it's like in Spanish. This one, the one that says permanent, *como permanente.*" I placed the auburn brown permanent hair dye along with all of my personal purchases on the counter and mumbled to myself, "Why do I always have to translate for you?" My mother flinched slightly, only in her shoulders, and only noticeable to me.

"Is that all?" asked the over-worked and under-paid cashier.

"Yes," I said.

"Tank you," my mother interjected. She paid for the supplies, grabbed the bag and walked out of the store with me trailing behind. We got in the car. She threw the bag in my lap, put the key in the ignition, and then slowly turned and looked at me. I turned the radio on. She turned it off.

"What?!" I said defiantly.

And in her perfect, deliberate Spanish she warned me,

"How you treat me now is exactly how your children will treat you. Remember *de tal palo, tal astilla.*" She had said the Spanish equivalent of "the apple doesn't fall far from the tree." Her eyes swelled with broken-hearted disappointed tears that would drown me with regret for the rest of my young adult life. I was ashamed of what I had done. Ashamed of what I said. Ashamed of how I had made her feel.

Turning sixteen didn't seem that important anymore. She had expected more from me. She had hoped that I would understand, but I had failed her that afternoon. I had pointed out her inadequacies and complained about them. I had treated her like the rest of the world did, and this she could not bear. She continued to cry. I dared not say a word. "*De tal palo, tal astilla,*" she repeated. *The apple doesn't fall far from the tree.* It rang like an incessant fire alarm in my ears. I felt a knot in my throat. I stared out the window. Blue bonnets, green grass, and periwinkle purple polish on my nails reflected in the window as my mother's anger and disappointment drove us home.

K-12Th Grade

What?! You speak Spanish?!
Yes.
But you're black!
I'm Dominican.
And they stare at me,
Confused.

Pelo Malo

"Ouch!" Jenny screamed like a dying a cat, "That hurts, Mami!"

"Ay, don't be so sensitive," Mami would say and slap the back of my sister's head with a wide-toothed comb.

If Mami wasn't cleaning, this was how every Saturday morning began or how every Sunday night ended. Jenny on the floor of the living room or me in a chair in the kitchen, Mami hovering over us with a bottle of hair grease, several combs, a frazzled bristle brush and several hundred bobby pins, rollers, rubber bands, and clips.

"Ay, este pelo tan malo," Mami would say. Jenny and I would roll our eyes, moan, groan and squirm in our seats for sometimes two or three hours at a time. The objective was always the same: to have hair that looked acceptable.

For *Dominicanas*, there are only two hair types: *pelo bueno* and *pelo malo*.

Good hair/*pelo bueno*: (noun). Hair that is straight, smooth and easy to manage. Hair found on a *Gringa*. The kind of hair most of us don't have. Sometimes, if your mother or the hairstylist is being nice, a soft curl that straightens easily is considered *"bueno"* too.

Bad hair/*pelo malo*: (noun). Any hair that resembles or reminds us of our African ancestry. It is what most of us have. Kinky, curly hair that requires relaxers, pins, pressing, excessive heat and grease. It is this kind of hair that is always treated with a scowl and a strong arm.

If you are cursed with *pelo malo,* as my sister and I both are, you are forced to relax it by the age of ten when wearing braids to school is no longer acceptable. It is the age when all the other girls start to wear their naturally straight hair down at the shoulders and you really want to fit in. So, you agree.

Relaxing is a chemical process. Relaxing destroys the natural kink and curl of the hair in an effort to make it more manageable. You believe this will make you prettier. You believe you will be able to blend in with the others now. You believe no one will notice you're different if your hair looks just like everyone else's. This is, after all, the best gift a girl can get: to feel just as beautiful as all the rest.

When you grow up hearing your mother, your *tías,* and every Dominican/Puerto Rican/Cuban hairstylist call your hair "bad," you inevitably start to develop a complex. You develop insecurities. You hate your hair. You are embarrassed by it. It consumes your Sunday nights. It prevents you from enjoying the pool, the park, the rain, or the snow. You do everything you can to make your bad hair "look" good. You try any and every product that promises to de-frizz, detangle, straighten, silken, manage, or mend your kinks and curls. Your hair is your obsession. Your hair is your arch nemesis. Your hair defies you and defines you. Your hair is never good enough.

That is until, one day you wake up and you rebel. If

you're lucky it happens at fifteen, sometimes at twenty or twenty-five, sometimes even at thirty. For some, it is not until their mother dies or they have a daughter of their own that they realize the damage these labels have caused. At this point, they will attempt to restore not only their split ends but their self-image as well. No more heat. No more chemicals. No more hot combs, curlers or cornrows.

You decide to go natural. Natural means no more chemicals. It means your hair the way God intended it to be. It means accepting your *Taíno* and African roots. If your mother, grandmother, *tías* and cousins are alive and around to see this process they will inevitably berate, belittle, question, comment, scowl and scold you for your decision. They are too set in their ways to understand your need to reclaim your identity.

> *¿Pero por qué?*

> *You look like a Haitian.*

> *What's with the Afro cuz?*

> *No me gusta.*

> *Wow! It's so BIG!*

> *Are you going to flat iron it or what?*

If you are strong enough, you survive the months of criticism and constant hair cutting. Because going natural is a process. You have two options: to dramatically chop it all off at once and look like you're recovering from chemotherapy or wait an incredibly long time for new hair growth to take the place of the old and slowly cut off the chemically-treated hair.

In the end, it is worth it, or so you hope. In the meantime, it is just another blow to your already damaged self-esteem. If you are not strong enough, you give in and you give up. You relax it again to shut everyone up or simply because natural isn't for you. You convince yourself that natural is more work and you don't have the time.

If you finally break through the agonizing transition, find the right natural hair care products and have a "good" hair day, you rejoice. You are not afraid of the rain or the weather. Your *Gringa* friends *ooh* and *ahh*. Everyone wants to touch it. You let them, at first. Your hair becomes the topic of conversation at social events. Everyone is jealous of your curl, of your kinks, of the way your hair sits on your head just so. You don't understand why it's taken you so long to embrace *your* hair. Your hair is no longer *pelo bueno* or *pelo malo*, it is just <u>your</u> *pelo*.

You begin to walk with a pep in your step and you and your hair get along more often now.

One day, your mother notices and decides to touch it.

"*Mira*, look at that. It's soft!"

Yes, it is, you think. You know that, from her, this is the closest you are going to get to a compliment; so, you smile and finally feel *beautiful*.

Jasminne Mendez

Show & Tell

It was Tuesday

Mr. Gleason asked us

To bring something

That would show

And tell the class

Something new

About our culture

And our identity

On Wednesday

I wore my father's

Military uniform

Tucked a Dominican

Flag in my pocket

Carried a rosary

Around my wrist

And told the class

Island of Dreams

Where I stand

Now

Is not where I was

Yesterday

Or where I will be from

The day after
Tomorrow

Jasminne Mendez

Home

You ask me where I'm from and I cannot give you an answer. Places to me are like the weather, unpredictable and ephemeral. I call no place home; I am from nowhere and everywhere. When you ask me of home, I have only this to say: *I remember little about where I've lived, only that I had to keep leaving.*

I grew up in five different houses and one apartment. Rooms and yards became the arbitrary holding cell for my family's stuff and for where we lived "in the meantime." I am able to say with certainty, that I do not miss any one home or room. I never allowed myself to become attached. I absorbed each yard by playing soccer in the wet grass with Linda, my imaginary friend, until she died and I had to bury her underneath the tool shed of the house in Louisiana. I climbed every tall and withered tree until my hands were calloused and *Mami* insisted I begin wearing skirts. I spent hours, in every white-walled room, writing about people and places I had never met until I was forced to go outside and make friends. No, the places are not what I long for; the harmonious, stress-free moments are what I miss the most.

When I wake up on Saturday mornings, my post-college one-bedroom apartment does not smell like Pine-sol® or *Fabuloso*®. I am not startled by the sound of a vacuum and no one is going to guilt me into making my bed. In the last few years, I have come to realize that I yearn for that kind of a Saturday morning. It never mattered what city we lived in, how big or small the house was, growing up I could always count on *Mami* to ruin a perfectly good marathon of Saturday morning cartoons. I would sit, eating my cold and soggy cereal on a stained and itchy carpet, and trying to enjoy Looney Tunes when *Mami* would inevitably mosey on in front of the dated television with Windex and a paper towel and start dusting.

"MAAA!!" I would scream. Her head would jerk back at me, eyes questioning my outburst. I would smack my teeth, sigh, and get up to help her. It never failed. Whether there were ten knick-knacks to dust or fifty, my mother's guilt-ridden eyes and angry cleaning sprees always left me holding a sponge and a bucket of dirty water.

I have tried with great effort to maintain my mother's cleaning habits, but it has proven impossible. I do not mop the way she does. I do not scrub *las ollas* the way she does. Something is always left stuck to the bottom of the pan, and I try desperately not to buy knick-knacks. Deep down, I know *Mami* meant well, and at least when I went away to college, I wasn't the "dirty roommate" thanks to her.

The inside of every house wasn't the only thing that had to be spotless. The yards, which were my father's area of expertise, were impeccable as well. In every house there was a garden to tend to and grass to mow. My brother was and is quite inept at hard labor, so I always took it upon myself to cut the grass when *Papi* was out of town for work. At ten, twelve, and fifteen years old I remember lacing up my tennis shoes, throwing on a pair of sweats, tying my hair back, and revving up a stubborn lawn mower that could have pushed me around more easily than I pushed it. As difficult as it often was, I enjoyed cutting the grass. The vibration of the engine against my hands tickled, and I reveled in the challenge of trying to lift the mower over the trunk of a tree to get the edges just right.

I can still smell the rainwater against the blades of grass that stuck to my legs. After each epic battle between my wimpy arms and the immortal lawn, I would reluctantly wash off the remnants of my victory and bask in the glory of my sun-kissed skin and hard work. I always felt accomplished after I mowed the lawn, even if it wasn't perfect, because I knew I had contributed something to the family. It also meant that my parents could spend less time cleaning and more time doing things with us as a family.The lawn, however, was not the only exterior portion of the house my parents insisted on cultivating. No, it seemed at times, that *Mami* and *Papi* took more pride in their fruit, rose, vegetable, "what is that anyway" gardens than in their own children's accomplishments. *Mami* and *Papi* have always pretended to be farmers. My father says he does this because he wants to reclaim his past. The time in his life when he lived on a plantation with goats, cows, snakes and wild fruit growing from trees and on uncultivated land. It is a time in the past, however, that no one else on his side of the family seems to remember.

My father plants orange trees in cities with climates that

are not meant to grow fruit, "Just to watch them grow," he says adamantly. "One day, you'll see, I'll come back, and that tree, that one, right there will be FULL of oranges. Just like when I lived *en el campo en Santo Domingo.*"

"But *Papi*," I reply, "You don't even remember *el campo*. You were like six when you moved to the city."

"Nooooo. I was eight." I laugh at him every time, because I desperately want to believe that one of these days he'll be right. Even though, we all know that oranges don't grow in Santo Domingo or New York.

Every Saturday morning, *Mami* would open the hose to water avocado seeds that would never give birth and feed rosebuds that betrayed her with thorns when she tried to pick them. To this day, *Papi* still invites family and friends over just to show them the four-foot apple tree that he is sure his grandchildren will eat from. The dream hasn't changed and neither has my father, even if the houses have come and gone. From sour lemons and limes, to overgrown tomatoes and imaginary grapes, my parents' green thumbs have scratched the dirt of every home that has had the privilege of housing the Rosario family.

I enjoyed every house in exactly the same way, with the indifferent acceptance of a stray cat being temporarily sheltered in a warm and loving place. It was not the house where we lived that mattered, but the fact that we were there together that did. No matter how many dishes cracked with each move and regardless of which room I was assigned to, I always knew that *Mami* would cook dinner, my sister and I would set the table, my brother would take out the trash, and *Papi* would fix anything that was broken.

I have lived in foreign countries where the air smells like beer and bratwurst. My mother thought she had made a permanent home for herself in a house with silent wooden floors and a voluptuous vegetable garden. I was enraptured by the house with my first walk-in closet. Yet none of those things seem to last, and my memories of what *home* is elude me as I desperately try to reconnect with places that only matter because my family still does.

War

I remember opening

One brown bag after another

Of Meals Ready to Eat hoping we'd find

Generic Kool-Aid®

To savor while we sat

On our cold basement floor.

Avoiding the powdered and packaged

Fake food, we drenched our

Fingers in purple and orange sugar

Instead. Laughing about it later on,

We wondered why no one

Had tried to stop us.

Every once in a while

Saturday nights belonged to

The joy of bubble wrap.

We would jump on it.

Easily amusing ourselves,

We didn't need candy or gifts

Or even attention.

The sound of simplicity

Popping underneath our toes

Was enough.

After each move I'd keep

As many cardboard boxes as possible

And I'd build a fortress

In my new bedroom.

In it I would store all the pieces

Of broken knick knacks, shattered

Toys and ruined books that didn't make it

From one state to the next.

It was my sanctuary of memories.

My only answer to the word *home*.

Sometimes, on the 4th

Of July, the planes would fly

High above our government provided

Housing and we would sit on the porch

And watch the fireworks explode above our heads.

Mostly though, the three of us

Spent time with mom.

Wishing *Papi* could have been there too.

Girl Talk

As children, teens and young adults, we were brought together for weddings, birthdays and holidays. Though our reunions were brief, our bond remains strong, because in Latin American families, cousins are like the cooler siblings you wish you could take home with you.

I have over fifty cousins on my mom and dad's sides combined. I only know about half of them. Growing up, I had a deeper connection with *Papi*'s side of the family than *Mami*'s, and as I think about it now, it's probably because we all grew up the same. On my father's side of the family, I have a total of five female cousins that I grew up with. Two of them came much after everyone else was already grown. Abigail and Altagracia were the oldest, and all of us younger females were expected to follow in their footsteps as smart, homemaking, God-fearing, and obedient women. That was until they both got divorced and Altagracia became a single mom and Abigail had to go back home and live with her mother. As little girls, my sister and I would play tea party with Abigail and Altagracia for hours on end. We would dress in our Sunday best and speak in our fanciest accents. Little pink and yellow dresses covered in white lace and satin ribbons adorned our bodies as we sipped on lemonade transformed into tea by the power of our imaginations. We talked about our imaginary trips to France and all the purses we would buy when we got there.

We were housewives and mothers from the very beginning. We cradled soft baby toys whose eyes blinked when you shook them, and enviously combed blond and brunette ringlets on pale skinned dolls. With each play session our older cousins taught us how to be who we were to become. They took pride in being our teachers, and we giggled with pleasure at each lesson we mastered. My sister and I both became very attached to Altagracia, the eldest, because she took the time to play with us and to listen to us, despite being twelve years older. She let us be children around her because that's all she still wanted to be.

As we all got older, however, our reunions became less about playing and having fun, and more about responsibility and work. Kitchens and dining rooms became our playground. Instead of playing with dolls, we chased roaches out of my *abuela's* and *Tía's* kitchens with *chanclas* and napkins. We danced clumsy *merengues* on the cold and stained linoleum floors and made a game of how to keep the plastic chair covers from sticking to our bottoms when we sat at the dining table to listen to the family gossip. We brewed hot Bustelo® coffee for our mothers on Sunday mornings and winced at the smell of fishy *bacalao* being cooked during Lent. While the boys and men found their sanctuaries in front of the television set or around a wooden table playing dominoes, we girls turned a monotony of chores into an amusement park with endless possibilities.

"¡Yamina, Irene, Jenni, Abigail, Altagracia, *vengan acá!* Set the table, and do it right this time. Call your brothers, *y dile a tu Papa.* And get the good plates out of the top drawer, no fake plates today."

"What are 'fake plates'?" I whispered to my cousin.

"Dixie," she'd reply and we would both laugh.

"*¿De qué se ríen ustedes?* Stop playing around and set the table already."

Unwillingly we would stand on small stools, grab heavy china out of cabinets, and like a factory line,proceed to set the table. We had a process, and often, just to keep us all sane, Altagracia and Abigail would erupt in song and dance and pretend we were all a part of some famous Broadway musical.

My cousin Abigail, who's the tallest, would stand on the stool, grab the plates, and hand them to Irene who was the fastest. The youngest, my sister Jenny, was in charge of the silverware, something she couldn't break, and Maria Elena, Maria Ana, and I were responsible for the cups and napkins. It was a common ritual that made our mothers proud, though they would never admit it.

Since the age of seven, I have always had to work for my food, all in preparation for what my parents consider my ultimate goal in life, to become someone's ideal Dominican housewife. Because of this, now if I go to a dinner party or BBQ or other event held at someone's house, I always help cook and clean and I always feel guilty when I don't or when I'm told not to. And let it be known that the guilt I feel is not like the average guilt one feels. No, what I'm talking about is even worse than Catholic guilt. It's Latina-mother guilt. The kind where she shakes her head, gets very angry with you and begins to curse in Spanish, saying phrases like *no seas malagradecida* OR *el que manda va dos veces* OR do what I told you already, which is then followed by something hard and dangerous flying past your head as you duck and cover.

Then, and only then, after she has threatened your life and her bout of anger and rage has come and gone like the wind, she will get teary eyed and start mumbling to herself things like "I've taken care of you all my life, *y mira*" or "what am I going to do with these children God, please, Jesus *ayúdame que no entiendo*." And she'll pick up a broom or a mop or a rag and start cleaning furiously, mumbling and crying incomprehensible curses. Which forces you to ask her, "*Mami*, what's wrong, what are you saying? What can I do? *Mami*?"

"*NADA! NADA!* I don't want you, or your brother or your sister, or even your father to do nothing. *No quiero NADA!*"

And you stand there in silence, with nothing to say until she tells you to leave, but you know you shouldn't, so you continue to stand there in silence. Eventually, you feel so sorry for her that you pick up a rag or a broom or a mop and you start cleaning around her, just to prove you're useful. But she stops you, and like a child recovering a stolen toy, she takes whatever it is you have out of your hands.

"Go, I'll do it myself. Leave it alone," she'll say.

"*Pero Mami,*" you'll begin and she'll cut you off.

"*YA!* Go away, I said I would do it!"

And you leave the room, feeling guilty. It's THAT kind of guilt. Since then, if it is not done right and if it is not done well, *that* guilt rises in my gut like a tsunami, washing away every other emotion and drowning my self-worth. And all because I didn't help the hostess at the party do the dishes.

Our enthusiasm for the homemaking process waned with each gathering and our roles changed with each new era. When Altagracia and Abigail were married and brought their husbands around, they were responsible for serving them while the rest of us were still expected to serve our fathers and brothers. Some, however, like Irene and my sister rebelled against this and insisted that, "They have two hands and two feet. They can serve themselves."

I was not so bold. I never dared complain or refuse. I had had enough objects fly past my head to know better. Deep down, I just wanted what Abigail and Altagracia had. If I was going to serve someone, I wanted it to be someone I had fallen in love with and that would appreciate me, and what I was doing for him.

Over the next few years, we bonded over real coffee, hot chocolate and late night girl talks where we bared our souls and shared our secrets about first loves and first times. It was during these nights that I would learn things about my sister she would never have told me on her own and that were important only because the rest of us could relate. We were able to share family gossip and discuss what we resented about our mothers and fathers, believing each of us had it worse than the others.

We didn't treat each other like cousins, we believed each other to be more like estranged sisters who had been reunited and couldn't wait to see again. Our journeys were different, but life would bring us together for some of our most precious moments and we knew we were forever united by blood. Each of us carries a story presumably different than the rest, but, ultimately, the same. We were and still are smart, strong, independent and passionate women. We want to make our families proud without sacrificing ourselves. And every day, we know that we must choose between the American dreams that live within us and the island dreams of our mothers.

Hollywood Dreams

How come no one

looks like me on TV?

Because they're from different

Latin American countries

No one has my skin color

No one my accent

They all sound Spanish

And look made of plastic

There's no woman I admire

No role model I can find

Just a sea of white faces

And black men

They don't seem to mind

Baseball players

And mad money chasers

Are my only inspiration

Demanding respect

*J*asminne *M*endez

Lacking education

No class

No style

Just light-skinned versions

Of Latinas gone wild

When I turn on the set

I try to forget

That my Hollywood dream

Isn't as hard as it seems

I just want to be on TV

So other girls can look up to me

Outsider

Of all the *primas* on *Mami's* side of the family, my sister and I were always the outsiders. My sister because she was the silent, brooding type, and in Dominican families no one is silent, and much less brooding. I was an outsider because I studied too hard and cared more about my grades and graduating than booty shorts and boys. While my *primas* were getting pregnant by players in real life, I was in theatre pretending to be pregnant women on stage. I took four AP classes at a time, played the alto saxophone, and never left school before 6:00 p.m. every day. My cousins said I thought I was *la gran cosa*. Too good for anyone or anything.

OOOhhh she's going to college in Hooousston, they mock.

But I got a scholarship, I say.

Oooohhh, somebody's paying HER to go to school, they snicker.

But I worked hard to earn those grades, I fight back.

Oooooh, she's so smart. She doesn't think our jokes are funny anymore, they get angry.

I've just heard them all before, I snap.

Every family dinner, BBQ, birthday party or holiday included the same questions and the same conversation. Why did Jasminne leave home for college? When is she coming back? Why doesn't she have a boyfriend? When is she getting married? Why is school taking so long? Doesn't she want to have kids?

How come you don't visit us in San Antonio anymore?

I'm really busy. I have a lot to study. It's hard to come out here on weekends.

But every time you come back you stay at your Mami's house, you don't visit us at our casas.

I know Tía. It's just I can only come for a weekend. It's hard to see everyone. It's easier if you all just come to Mami's house.

Humph, our little casitas are humble but they're clean. It wouldn't hurt you to come visit US some time.

I'm sorry. I will.

And I do make an effort, but even so, my inability to connect with my *tías* and *primas* continues. While they club-hopped and cooed their babies, I went to poetry readings and traveled to Paris. I earned two degrees in five years, while they earned a GED and bought a used car. They laugh loud at everything and complain about their hips while eating a plate of fried plantains and *habichuelas guisadas*. Our priorities are different, our paths in life not the same.

So, Jas, when are you moving back home? My cousin asks.

Oh, I'm not.

Why?! You're done with school aren't you?

Yes, but I like Houston.

Oh.

What?

Nada. You just act like you hate <u>all this</u> so much.

What are you talking about?

You think you're better than us.

No, I just want to do more with my life than have babies.

Being a mother is the best job in the world.

Yeah, but it doesn't pay the bills. And I don't want to have to depend on a man the rest of my life.

And what's wrong with that?

It's just not for me.

And I leave the room, and eventually the house, and the city, feeling like an outsider every time.

Jasminne Mendez

Foundation

My dirt, *Mi tierra*

As seen by the eyes of an outsider

is poor, sad and desperate.

Bleak, broken and desolate.

My people, *Mi gente,*

Live with no running water

the heat of the sun burning and tainting

their Spanish-colored flesh

into Haitian, Jamaican, African soul.

The trees echo the cries of starving children

and the sorrows of fallen women.

But My dirt, *Mi tierra*

is much more than a third-world country

on the verge of cultural assimilation

and dissipation.

It is drum beats keeping rhythm with heartbeats.

It is a three-stringed guitar playing

old-school Bachata.

Es una güira adding flavor to a two-step Salsa.

My dirt, *Mi tierra*

Needs not the sweat of *mis tíos* and *mis abuelos*

drenching the parched, putrid pavement.

Or the "¡*Agua de coco, dos pesos, Agua de coco, dos pesos!*"

Suffocating the streets of *el malecón*.

It can survive without five star resorts,

foreign tourists and the colonization of

Mickie D's, KFC's, and SUV's.

It can thrive on the fresh mangos falling from trees.

Los plátanos verdes deep fried in grease.

And the sweet, strong taste of *Mama Juana*.

Santo Domingo,

Santiago,

y Puerto Plata

Pulsate and radiate.

Stagnate and disintegrate.

The song of these people is heard inside *la bodega*

on the hills of *el campo*

and on the rooftops of *el barrio*.

"¡*Ojalá que llueva café en el campo!*"

¡*Sí*, YES! *que caiga un aguacero de yuca y te*.

Let fall from the sky food, hope, and new dreams

so that all may be fed.

Give them a name and a face.

A religion of strength and decision.

My dirt, *Mi tierra*

Runs wild with *mujeres en la calle*,

hombres emborrachados,

and barefoot boys batting baseballs with broomsticks

en el ensanche.

My dirt, *Mi tierra*

Is rich with *cultura*

and deprived of *justicia*.

Island of Dreams

My people, *Mi gente*

Remain seated on the seesaw of

ignorance and independence.

But even with all their pain and sorrow,

there is one thing from America these people

do not need to borrow.

Because you see,

My dirt, *Mi tierra*

fully understands *que,*

"No hay que llorar

porque la vida es un carnaval

y las penas se van, cantando."

And although

The land, the music,

the colors of the flag

Dios

Patria

y Libertad is all they have,

Life

Love

Freedom

y Esperanza

courses through the veins of

Santo Domingo,

Santiago,

y Puerto Plata.

The Cause

He slams his calloused hand down on the table and waves a paperback book in my face. Then, with a stern sigh of despair he says, "This, *this* is what I came to this country for." Instinctively I know what he means. He came for knowledge. He came for the freedom to live as he wanted and to take care of his family on his own terms. Finally, after twenty-two years in America, he wanted to believe that he had accomplished just that. Yet he stood there, asking me with his eyes and a tattered copy of *The Third Reich,* at what cost had he achieved the American dream? At what cost?

When my father lived in Santo Domingo, he rebelled and protested in the streets. He hated politics, racism, favoritism, and any red, white, and blue flag that did not bear the Dominican seal. He used to march the streets stepping left, right, right, left in no particular order. It was organized chaos and misinterpreted rage at its finest. Month after month and year after year my father could be found screaming and forever believing: "¡*Viva la revolución*! ¡*Viva la revolución!*" As long as there was a political opinion he could contradict, he did it. The Dominican military beat, bruised, and attempted to mace and erase my father and his friends out of history. But his Communist regalia and coffee house manifestos for *la causa* and *la raza* could not be ignored.

His cause, the cause of his country was to better its people. *Su gente.* He wanted his people to be free from the restraints of poverty. He wanted a better life for his single mother who was forced to raise six children in a two-bedroom shanty. He wanted school to be a necessity and not a luxury. For these and many other causes, when he wasn't selling hot fresh bread or prepping bodies in the school morgue for a few *pesos* a day, he was spilling his sweat in the streets.

My father wore heavy combat boots, freedom inspired jeans, and a fist full of pride that would lead those behind him into an unfortunate land of hope and unfulfilled *promesas*. He and his *colegas* marched away their anger, looted for the love of their people, lived, breathed and spoke for the cause that dripped from their pores. He believed, then, that his country was headed for better days and he wanted nothing more than to see it through.

But he did not. He could not. Because youth and desire do not last forever. Time interrupted my father and got in the way of his passion. My father was offered the opportunity of a green card and five years later he found himself marching to the beat of a different drummer. A foreign drummer. A march provided by Uncle Sam and the red, white and blue stars and stripes of America. The synchronized, capitalized, left, right, left, right steps of *los Estados Unidos.* He left Santo Domingo because other promises were made. He made a promise to my own mother, his wife, that he would love her, protect her, and provide for her. Promises that he kept by enlisting in the Army and never mentioning the revolution again.

*I*sland of *D*reams

After two decades in the U.S., he realized that he had marched to the structured and ruptured steps of America so long that he had been forced to believe in party politics. The boots he had worn carried him further off the island and planted his soles deeper into the ground of assimilation. He learned the foreign language that stuck to his mouth like peanut butter and he sent his kids to school out of necessity and pride. His cause had changed and yet somehow remained the same.

Over the last twenty years, my father had gone to war, come back from war, and had to suffer and give to a country he had previously only read about. He knew there was a cause for those wars, but it was not his cause, and it was not for his people. His raised fist has been replaced by an empty hand holding an invisible dream, asking me, what for? Was it all in a valiant but futile effort to preserve the freedom of someone else's native land? I see him now, holding onto his desperate pride and anxious hope. I look up at him and back down at the book he is holding. I'm trying to find an answer in the space that lies between them, but I am at a loss. I don't know what this grown man needs from me and even if I did I don't know that I want to give it to him. We have just returned from our first trip back to the island after nineteen years, and my father, the strong military man is almost in tears. While we were there, my father took us all on a day trip back to his old university. The place where he once fought the good fight when he still believed in something. He took us there to find his cause, to see the outcomes of his protests, and to understand *his* revolution. When we arrived, all he found was a wall with a faded inscription: *La Juventud Comunista de Santo Domingo.* The Society of Young Communists of Santo Domingo does not exist on campus anymore it has become nothing more than a slab of stone weathered by years of forgotten ideas. It is now a talking point for the young revolutionaries that idolize Che but can't stomach Castro. It is nothing more than a tourist spot for hipster Europeans. My father didn't know what to say as he searched the wall for more, and we didn't know what to expect. Instead, he handed my mother the disposable camera, smiled and just took a picture.

He is staring at the picture now and trying to make sense of the last thirty years of his life. I take the relic from his hand, place it inside the book he has inadvertently threatened me with, and I hug him gently. He grunts and wipes his glasses. I place my hand on his shoulder and I tell him, "Pa, I'm applying for graduate school next fall."

He smiles again. His cause.

Juan Luis Guerra

Somewhere
On a beach in Santo Domingo
Jesus is writing love poems
Making love to Spanish
And dancing with a woman
The world has never met

The Music

And those who were seen dancing were thought to be insane by those who could not hear the music.

-Frederic Nietzsche

I like to dance salsa, *merengue*, *bachata*, hip-hop, pop, anything, really. I like it when my hips sway. My legs and feet often stumble to the beat, but I can feel the rhythm, the soul, and the passion of the music. I can twirl and shake for hours. Whether I'm cleaning the house, at a club, drunk or sober, I like to dance. I just need to feel the bass, the guitar, and the drums. The drums that beat like a schoolgirl in love.

When I was a little girl, *Mami* would always play Juan Luis, Julio Iglesias or La India on our record player and clean the house from top to bottom. Since then, I have always known the importance of music to my family, my culture and *mi gente*. I know that the soulful rhythms, reminiscent of a simpler life back in the DR, are what kept my mother sane most days. Without those mournful voices and synchronized tambourines, I'm sure she would have packed a bag, left a note and walked out the door like so many other desperate housewives of her time did. But deep inside she knew how to let Jerry Rivera and Los Hermanos Rosario keep her heart alive and her spirit free.

Unfortunately for me, however, *Mami*'s strong beating heart meant that I would be awakened every Saturday morning by a humming vacuum, a *güira,* a guitar and some Caribbean man's achy voice complaining about some *maldita mujer* that had left him for another man. *Mami* would then eventually scream "¡*Levántate de ahí ya!*" And our Saturday morning cacophony of sounds and chores would begin.

I'd reply, "But why?!" And carefully, but deliberately, she'd come to my bed, snatch off the covers, and say, "*Porque yo dije,* because I said so." I would then oblige, get up, and commence the monotonous job of dusting and scrubbing, as a scratchy merengue rocked the house and my mother back and forth.

The cleaning, singing and missed-step dancing became a ritual in our house that lasted more than 10 years. The sounds of our home vibrated through our walls and under our feet. It made us laugh. It made us angry. It was a silent prayer, a requiem for deferred dreams and an uncertain future. Amidst my mother's nagging and my teenage rebellion, it was the only way we knew how to make peace. If she was disappointed in me or if I was angry with her, all she had to do was play a soft merengue, offer me a mop and a bucket of water, and suddenly all was forgiven. I knew my place and so did she, but we could always count on the music to bring us together.

I knew then, as I know now, that music is essential to the

well-being of my family and my culture. I know that dancing is crucial and necessary for our survival. The lyrics tell the stories of who we are and the beat grounds our heart and soul in a land that isn't and never will be ours. I know that both define who we are as a people and a race. I know that even if school or work or life get too busy, I, like my mother always did, still can and should find the time, the energy, and the spirit to hear the music and *dance.*

Family Secrets

I

"but you chose <u>me</u>," she wrote

and I fold it back up

knowing I've read too much

letters from *Mami* to *Papi*

II

a photograph is ripped in half

lipstick smeared on the sofa

a *comadre* sits in silence

my mother offers her a cup of coffee

and a prayer

III

whispers over the phone

a strange man comes to the door

my father calls us to the kitchen

"you've never seen this much money before"

IV

he drinks with his friends

he hollers

she yells

he sleeps in

she works late

leaves bruises on her face

a suitcase by the door

they take her away

he always comes crawling back

V

dessert storm, war, 1991

pictures and postcards

bullets and broken bones

I wonder why

Papi doesn't sleep at night

VI

the other woman

has his baby

my *Tía* still cooks him dinner

VII

tu Tío is paranoid, why?

tu Tía is sick, with what?

tu Prima is pregnant, by whom?

your cousin is dead, which one?

VIII

Mami mumbles something about *el vicio*

grandma falls quietly to the floor

he's pawned everything in the house

and cannot be found

anymore

IX

a bathtub full of water

an empty bottle of pills

she cries herself to sleep

her sisters take the children

and leave

X

I listen well

I don't ask

I don't tell

I keep a shoe box of memories

and moments

Hidden

Safe inside of me

Jasminne Mendez

Souvenirs

My ex-boyfriends are scars. I take them with me wherever I go, and each one is its own personal story that taught me something. I was not so nice to some of my exes. Some were not so nice to me. I cheated, and I was cheated on and it hurt like heartbreak always does. The beginning of each relationship was always the same. Yet, it was the end that I anticipated with reckless anxiety and always avoided until letting the tears fall felt better than faking a smile. I ended each relationship with either one destructive blow or with reluctant apathy. Never wanting or needing to get too close.

For every man/boy/child that I fell in love with, I became who I thought he wanted me to be. Afraid of my own color, I disbelieved that these men could truly see my external beauty. My hair was not smooth, my nose was too wide, and my butt too small for a Latina. My body defied me. I was no one's stereotype. So instead, I learned to become the woman any man would want on the inside. I hid behind books, music, intellect, culture, food and genuine love, hoping that no one would notice I was brown. After all, who could really fall in love with a pseudo Latina black girl from nowhere who spoke Spanish and had frizzy hair? But many did fall in love with me, even if I eventually pushed them away.

Over the last few years, however, my culture has begun

to bleed through my eyes. I am not like my white friends. I don't dance like my black friends. The Puerto Ricans don't roll their "r's" like I do, and the Mexicans call their *habichuelas, "frijoles."* Which is something I will never get used to. I see now, however, that my experience matters, that my Dominicanness is a story with a few well-earned scars.

I know now, that if I keep avoiding the Afro-Latino elephant in the room, I will become a lie in a society that has already been ignoring me for centuries. This is something I can no longer allow. So, with my harsh gestures and broken Spanish, I have made everyone listen to the Caribbean and Taíno drums that beat inside me and echo from my pores. I now hang a Dominican flag from the rear view mirror of my car, refuse to be identified as a Mexican, and fry plantains for my friends at dinner parties merely to prove my own authenticity. But there are days when I don't know if it's working. I don't know if *this* relationship, the one I have with myself, has the potential for growth, or if I'll ever be ready to commit.

It is this strained relationship that I have with myself, with the color of my skin and the texture of my hair that has scarred me the most. I can't keep tucking my identity away in a drawer like an unwanted souvenir. I can't break up with me, but I am tired of cheating on myself. I must eventually reconcile the differences between my American self and my Dominican self. I realize now, that I must let them fall in love with each other before I can ever let any man fall in love with me.

Jasminne Mendez

Poetry

The words in my head
Cause multiple spasms on my tongue
Before they are said

Because the purpose of my
Poignantly predictable yet powerful
Poetry
Is not to be recorded in history
But etched in the memory
Of everyman, every woman
Who chooses to listen actively
Rather than passively placing
My book
On a shelf

A shelf too small for *my* book,
Because my book is not a book,
It is an idea
An idea too soon for its time
But not considered one of a kind
Because no one wants to hear the story

Of a Latina anymore

We're just the victim

The mother of ten

Pregnant at fifteen

Yet always the beauty queen

The woman who can't seem to leave her

Wife-beating man

But why can't anyone seem to understand

That without him:

My children would starve

My book will tell the truths

Of every over-tested

Under-stimulated

Low-income

At-risk minority child

That has already been left behind

My book will be an afterthought

At dinner parties for the rich who

Presumptuously presume to know

What my book is

Really all about

An angry, raging,

Overly sensitive

Wanna-be, never gonna be

Recognized

Poet

Trying to cope with her own

Inadequacies

By pointing out the majorities

But what they'll fail to see

Is that while they waited for the revolution.

My poetry *is* the revolution

And this revolution can be found

Only in the mind

Rarely written on paper

Paper

Notebook paper

Tissue paper

"Where are your papers?"

"*¿Dónde están MIS papeles?*"

"Where are your papers?"

Asks the officer again as

He begins the process of my

Deportation and excommunication from

My homeland

Because the only papers I carry

Tell of who I am

But only from my perspective

Not *la ley, la migra,* or *el estado's*

Expectation

Because I've come to the realization

That my poetry is the barbaric yawp

That I will sound from all the rooftops

Of the world

Because it is the only way I can be sure

My words *will* echo!

Florida Water

Growing up, we used it to make saints of ourselves, to make us holy, and to make us whole. We poured it on ceramic statues or on our bodies to heal the knots made by demanding parents and illusionary ancestors. The water was used to satisfy the thirst of the skeletons in our overcrowded closets and scare away demons we had only dreamed about.

As I got older, it would rain over my sorrows and caress my grandmother's dying diabetic legs every night before she laid them to rest. During rainy winter nights, I would see the shadow of my *Tía* kneeling next to a homemade altar and worshiping guardian angels that only laughed while she cried as my uncle slept his addictions away. She would then pour this holy water into a bowl next to a candle that would burn for days in a futile attempt to save both their souls.

My mom called my aunt's candle-lit praying and sobbing *brujería,* or witchcraft. Yet she always crossed herself every time she walked passed the ominous table covered with wax and remorse. My aunt claimed the altar was a symbol for the age-old belief that everything in life would turn out fine *si Dios quiere,* if God wills it.

Deep inside we all knew that our superstitions could cure the healthy, but would always keep the hungry poor. And these rituals and beliefs along with many others came with this cologne, this special water, which was wrapped in a bottle, packaged in Jersey, shipped to New York, and labeled Florida Water. Florida water, the holy potion, feel good, cure-all.

Have shoulder pain? Florida Water.

Feeling depressed? Florida Water.

Tienes gripe? Florida Water.

Have a prayer? Florida Water.

Need a *milagro? Agua Florida.*

I thought this water was God's medicine until the age of nineteen. At nineteen I stood in my dorm room afraid. I was too afraid to move and too afraid to think. Life was moving fast, with new people, big ideas, so much to learn, so much to do, and someone to become. Yet my inner spirit seemed to be sleeping. Who was I? What was I doing? What did it all matter?

I called my mom and I told her, "Mom, my back aches from the weight I have to carry. Mom, my legs hurt from walking so far. Mom, my arms feel empty. Could you send me a bottle?"

I thought that all I needed was a bottle of Florida Water to soothe away my aches and pains and to clear my mind of its identity fog. And so she sent it. She sent a clear plastic bottle. Shaking and trembling, it scarcely made its way through handling and shipping. Fragile was my state, and home was marked on the box it came in.

It came, and I showered with it. I believed every inch of my being would now be saved. I felt freedom rescue my fear and loneliness, and it made me laugh. My body began to sanction ghosts and beckon lost childhood memories as the weight of all my faults trickled down the wet tiled floor. I stared at my feet and began to remember the paths that I had traveled and why I had come to be where I was. I heard whispers of something vacant and far. Suddenly the smell of repentance, of mint leaves, of something holier than me lingered in my hair. Miracles now spoke to me in a foreign tongue that I had once refused to understand. My family's ancestry suddenly became a footnote in the history book I realized I had never bothered to read.

My body shook, and I dropped the bottle of Florida water. My only hope of redemption spilled all over the bottom of the shower. As I reached for the bottle, I saw the word "cologne" printed in black letters on its label. It was then, that I realized that the water was not the savior I had expected. I understood then that the water was only scented water, and only became more because my family willed it so. I realized in that moment, when my hand embraced the trophy of false altars and broken promises, that in the search to find myself I had forgotten my blood and my history and only found myself alone. I was attempting to achieve dreams my parents had worked for, and trying desperately to build a future with no regard for my past.

I had gone away to college to be able to be myself. But a part of who I was, was found in them, and I could no longer keep running from it. I went home that weekend hoping my eyes would beg for forgiveness so my mouth would not have to. I hugged *Mami* and told my father I loved him. That same weekend after Sunday breakfast my father told us he wanted us to be more like a family again. He felt we were all going our separate ways and he didn't want us to forget each other. It was the first time I had ever seen him cry.

In that moment, it was the water he shed from his eyes that healed me and not the Florida Water that I had begged for and showered with. I finally saw *Mami* and *Papi* as human. In that moment, they were and had always been, just a man and woman doing the best they could with what they had. In that moment, Florida Water had inadvertently given me something more than just a miracle; it had given me understanding.

Jasminne Mendez

El Profesor

There is a picture of a man

Holding a glass of whiskey.

He is smiling

And laden with sweat.

He wears a green *guayabera*

Unbuttoned.

His eyes look tired

But alive.

The picture sits

On an altar

In *Mami*'s house.

And this,

Is all I know

Of my grandfather.

Island of Dreams

Santo Domingo Smiles

This is not my story to tell.

It is her life and only she knows the truth behind it.

But my mother's tongue belongs to the island.

If she were to tell you what she knows

Her cloudy English would make it all seem like a lie

And you would hate her for betraying what you think

Sunny island days and juicy mango nights are supposed to be like.

So, I will purposefully fail to do my research

For fear of opening wounds that would leak poverty and salt water;

Instead, I will piece together this story by collecting abandoned pictures,

By spying on the memories of clanky coffee cup Sunday mornings,

And by reading stolen letters written in a language even my mother has forgotten.

I want to send her home so she can smile again.

I want to have the money to build her a big house in el campo,

With a generator that will always work

And with water pipes that will never leak so she can feel at peace again.

But I know, that even if I did she would defy me like a spoiled child

Because my mother cannot be still.

I know this because of her erratic cleaning sprees at 3:00 a.m.

I know this because she is compelled to mop the kitchen every day.

I know this because the picture of her, wearing tight leather pants straddling a motorcycle reveals to me that she was and still wants to be

Adventurous.

She believes in a God that is merciful, but she doesn't understand the pain or the poverty.

She met my father and fell in love with hope and opportunity.

He left her alone for boot camp, in a dark, damp city where she cried herself to sleep

Holding his letters that promised brighter days to come.

She built the heart of a home with a bottle of bleach, a frying pan, and a Rosary.

Her alma bleeds for her Americanized children and her tears rain on palm trees she cannot see.

If she loved someone before *Papi*, I will never know.

If she had bigger dreams of fame and fortune I will never know.

If she wanted to be something more than just my mother, I don't have the courage to ask.

And if I could send her back to the Santo Domingo

That used to smile on her olive skin and make her laugh, I would.

But that island doesn't exist anymore,

Only her memories of something else do.

I don't want to let her down, but she needs more than what I can give her.

She needs fresh coconut milk to nourish her soul like holy water

So she can believe again.

She needs fresh ocean breezes to tickle her neck so she can feel young again.

She needs the dance of a live merengue to rock her to sleep so she can dream again.

My mother longs for the past like she fears for the future,

Watching her family come and go apart.

Praying in silence, believing in miracles, and always feeling

Like she left herself behind.

And yet, I must remember that *this* is not *my* story to tell.

Change

Mami and *Papi* had to save, wait, and budget for over twenty years before they had a chance to return to the island. There was never enough money or time to pack up three kids and two adults and spend hundreds of dollars just to take a vacation back home. The trip was emotional for all of us. I had waited nineteen years to see a place I had only dreamed of or Googled about. My mother hadn't been back since *Papito,* her father, had died when I was born and my father was last seen there hopping from the courthouse to the airport after he married *Mami* to get started on her Green Card paperwork back in New York.

We were all excited and nervous. We all had expectations the island could neither satisfy nor erase. For my parents, Santo Domingo was nothing like they remembered. It seemed smaller, more crowded, loud and unkempt. For my siblings and me, it was paradise and it was poverty but it finally felt like at least a part of us belonged somewhere.

"This is so cool," I said. "I'm so excited to finally be going!" I rushed through the airport clutching my suitcase with excitement as *Mami* told me to slow down.

"*Cálmate,* there's no rush. We'll get there."

"I know, but I can't help it! I want to be there already." She smiled at me and we both knew we felt the same thing. My relationship with *Mami* had changed drastically in the last year since I went away to college. We finally had a chance to miss each other. We didn't fight anymore because we needed each other more. She missed me like only a mother can and I loved her unconditionally like only a child does. We spoke on the phone every day and shared secrets like best friends. We still had our differences, but we understood each other better now. We respected each other as women because I had finally become one, and I realized that that's what she had been waiting for.

I normally fall asleep on plane rides, car rides, and road trips down the street, but this time I had too much nervous energy. I stared out the window, fidgeted with a magazine and reapplied makeup at least five times. I couldn't sit still and my face hurt from smiling so much. When the plane finally landed, I cried. My history, my family's past and my identity finally felt real. Santo Domingo wasn't just an illusion or a faded photograph anymore. It was a real place with real people, and they all looked and sounded like me. My brother jumped around anxiously in his seat, and Jenny, in her usual apathetic way said, "It's nice."

Stereotypically dressed men and women in *guayaberas*, flowing red and blue skirts, and drums and a guitar, greeted us with song and dance. We were undoubtedly considered tourists and were treated just so, but my goal was to change that by the end of the trip. I may have not been born there, but I felt and wanted to be just as Dominican as the next *Quisqueyano*. I didn't want to be spoken to in broken English or handed piña coladas. I wanted to hear loud Spanish thrown at me from across the *barrio* and to buy a *frío-frío* off of some guy's truck in the middle of a hot summer day. If I forced people in America to understand I was *Dominicana*, I wanted to be sure I lived up to that standard while on the island.

My cousin picked us up from the airport and drove us to our hotel in downtown Santo Domingo to drop off our bags.

"How was the flight?"

"*Bien*, good. It was very easy for us," my father replied.

"That's because you have a blue passport." My cousin was referring to the fact that everyone knew if you had a "blue" or American passport you were treated better at the airport and at Customs. Your bags didn't get searched, Security smiled at you politely and no one patted you down. It wasn't a fair practice, but it was just the way it was.

After several winding roads and a few close calls with motorcyclists in heavy traffic, we arrived at our hotel. We washed up, changed clothes, and within a few minutes we were whisked away to my Grandmother's house *en el ensanche*.

My maternal grandmother's house isn't anything to brag about. But she's owned it for over thirty years and in the DR that counts for a lot. The house is a small two-story shanty made of cement and dirt with a leaky tin roof. It sits on the middle of a hill attached to other shanties each one painted a different color. My grandmother's house is bright green with a small porch and a wrought iron spiral staircase that leads up to the second floor.

When I walked into her home I was reminded of the shotgun houses I'd seen in New Orleans on my last trip there. From the front door step you could see all the way to the back alley behind the kitchen. To my right was a small TV and a dining table, to my left a love seat. Not five feet in front of me was a bathroom and a small bedroom, and two steps to the left and three feet back was a stove, an ice chest and a big tub of water. Upstairs, there was one large open space with three beds and a dresser. It was small. It was humble, but it was what my mom called home. This is where my mom, her parents and nine other siblings grew up. I suddenly choked on all the ungrateful words I had ever uttered at my parents about what they had or hadn't done or bought for me.

"*¿Qué crees?* What do you think?" *Mami* asked.

The only thing I could muster up the courage and dignity to say was, "What's the large bucket of water for, *Mami*?"

"That's the water for the day. It's what they use to cook and take a shower with." She pointed to a small corner at the back of the kitchen that had a drain on the floor and what looked like a shower curtain hung on the wall. "They heat the water on the stove from this tub and take a couple of buckets to bathe with. *Y ya*. That's it."

I was in shock. I mean I knew people lived like this. I just didn't realize *my* people had to, especially in the city, where I assumed everything was modernized and new.

"Ma, they don't have running water? I thought that was

only in *el campo*. How come you and *Papi* didn't tell us that? You only told us about the *apagones*, about the lights always going out. I didn't know you had to bathe like this."

"*Ay*, I don't know. I guess we didn't want to think about it anymore. You try to forget about the bad stuff when you get the good stuff. Besides, when it's the only thing you know, you think it's normal. Anyways, *no importa*. Let's eat some lunch. Aren't you hungry?" I was famished. Despite the fact that I believed my family to be in an impoverished state, when I returned to the dining/living room, the table was covered with the most amazing Dominican food I had ever seen. *Arroz con habichuelas, tostones, pastelitos, pollo guisado, ensalada de papa* and a cold red soda in a glass bottle for each of us. I was in food heaven and I devoured all of it. Even if the light bulbs didn't work and you were only allowed to flush the toilet twice a day to save water, these people, *my* people sure did know how to cook.

"*¿Les gustó?*" Grandma asked.

"*Sí,*" we all replied and rubbed our bellies in satisfaction.

Shortly thereafter, aunts, uncles, cousins, second cousins, neighbors, great aunts, great uncles, *comadres*, and *compadres* and *la Cristiana* from down the street arrived and bombarded us with questions. Hugs, kisses, stories of my parent's childhood and photo albums were passed around like a game of hot potato. I felt overwhelmed and elated all at once. There were so many things I learned about and had always been too afraid to ask.

Your father's nickname was el loco because he found a snake once, chased it, and killed it with a hatchet.

Your mother only weighed ninety pounds when she left for Nueva Yol.

Your parents used to sit on that porch and only hold hands and talk for hours at a time.

Your father sold bread on the corner to pay for schoolbooks.

Your mother worked in the city as a secretary and thought she was too good for us.

Your grandfather was el professor, and everyone respected him.

Your father worked in the morgue while in college and wrote poetry about politics.

We thought you guys would never come back.

It's been too long.

There were facets of my own personality, interests, likes and dislikes that I finally began to understand. My love for poetry finally made sense, though I had never seen or heard *Papi* read or recite it himself. I now knew that teaching was in my blood and that my parent's courtship was sweet, tender, and nothing like I had imagined. I felt validated and cheated all at once.

How did I not know these things?

Why had they been kept from me?

What else was I missing?

When my parents finally decided that they had had enough and needed to rest, my cousin drove us back to the hotel. My grandmother had tried to insist we stay at the house, but my parents refused, blaming their Americanized children's desire for comfort and luxury. On the way to the hotel my brother and sister continued to probe my parents for answers. I was too tired, and too emotionally confused and spent to keep talking. I stared out the car window and tried to make sense of the men on the streets, the barefoot children, the tin roofs, the mopeds and the McDonald's and of the fact that even here, I still felt like a foreigner.

As we pulled up to the hotel, my cousin started laughing. "*Mira ese guachimán* sleeping over there. He's not even doing his job." My *primo* was pointing to the security guard who was sleeping in a chair with his mouth wide open and a hat over his eyes in the front of our hotel.

"*Primo*, what did you just call him?" I had never heard the word *guachimán* before.

"*Qué, guachimán?*"

"Yes. What is that?"

"Well, it's like in English "watching man," *porque* he's the man who watches. *Guachimán*. Well he's supposed to watch *pero* this guy *no está haciendo na'*.

I started laughing. We all started laughing. It was a word

none of us had heard before and an obvious distortion of both languages. I began to feel at ease knowing that we were all experiencing some culture shock together as a family. I felt I wasn't alone on this journey anymore and that we all had something to discover about our island, our past, and ourselves.

For the next two days, we visited family, historical landmarks, museums and neighborhoods my parents were nostalgic for. *Papi* showed us the street corner where he was arrested for protesting and *Mami* bragged about how once upon a time she worked in the city for a *licenciado*. At night, my cousins showed us the town and taught us how to eat *chimichurris* from a guy off a truck at a car wash crowded with SUVs playing loud *merengues* until five in the morning. The two days following all of that were spent in the hotel room nursing our upset stomachs. One by one, our sensitive Americanized intestines gave out and rejected the street food we had consumed in a forty-eight hour period. The only one of us who didn't get sick was *Mami*. She had always been a picky eater and had warned us,

"*Les estoy diciendo*, they don't cook with the same grease here like they do in the states. Be careful what you eat. Your stomachs can't handle it. You're going to get sick." We all thought she was overreacting and being snooty. Wanting to consume the island and all its flavors whole, we ignored her. My father, who could eat anything under the sun and not get sick, took our side.

"Let the kids eat what they want. It's their first time here, they need to experience it all." And we did experience it *all,* including the runs. My cousins laughed at our irritated bowels and my grandmother made a homemade *sancocho* to soothe our achy stomachs. By day five, we were back on the road headed to *el campo* to visit more family and get eaten up by mosquitoes. I tried to appreciate the hilly mountainside, the exotic fruit, and the three underfed goats my father insisted he remembered, but I couldn't get past the heat and the humidity, the bugs and the bad smells. I met distant relatives, took a few photos and sat in our rental car for the remainder of the stay. I complained my stomach still hurt and that I needed to lie down, so I was left alone.

While lying in the car, I thought about what my life could have been like had I grown up on the island. Would I have had the same opportunities or less? I know *Papi* would have made sure we got a good education no matter what, but would I have been so inspired to study the arts and literature? Perhaps seeing the poverty and experiencing it on a day-to-day basis would have moved me to study something more useful and practical, like medicine or law. Or, maybe not. Would I have run off with some *tiguere* and gotten pregnant just to spite my parents or would I have had dreams of moving to America like everyone else? I didn't know. I knew I would never know. I had to accept that. As I thought about the last four days I realized how fortunate I was in some ways and impoverished in others. I had everything I physically needed and more in the states but I was missing the sense of peace you get from knowing "where you're from." I didn't feel grounded on either soil. No matter how well I spoke English or Spanish or how many plantains or potatoes I fried, I and all of us who were born over *there* of parents from over *here,* were our own island. We were islands floating around displaced in space and time between here and there trying to make sense of the word *home.*

After a while, my sister came and joined me in the car.

"You had enough too?" I asked.

"Hell yes. I can't stand these bugs and it's too hot," she scratched her legs and wiped the sweat off her nose.

"What are they doing in there anyway?"

"Telling stories and drinking coffee. What else?"

"I'm ready to be on a beach somewhere."

"Me too."

"So what do you think so far?" I was hoping to have a deep conversation about my internal identity crisis, but I knew I was expecting too much from Jenny.

"It's fine," and she leaned her head against the passenger seat window.

"I mean do you like it? Is it what you thought?"

"It's ok, I guess. It's hot." She sighed and closed her eyes. I knew the conversation was over.

"I wish they'd hurry up," I said, and I too closed my eyes and sighed.

My less than pleasurable experience in *el campo* was vindicated by the last three days of the trip, which were spent at a resort in Bávaro. I had had a genuinely great time in the city exploring the complicated history of my parent's past, but I was ready to enjoy the paradise I had been promised. While at the resort, I spent hours by the pool and the sea re-reading, ironically enough, *The Great Gatsby* and drinking piña coladas. I had given in to the tourist trap and a part of me was happy to concede. My parents were grateful that they could share this side of the island with us but I knew they mourned for the Santo Domingo they had grown up in.

"*Mami*, do you miss it here?" I put my book down on the last afternoon of our visit and stared out into the ocean.

"*Bueno*, I did, at first. When I first moved to *Nueva Yol* I missed the island terribly, because everything there was so cold and so dark. And trust me, my mother-in-law was not an easy woman to live with. Your father left for basic training and I felt so alone. I wanted nothing more than to come back home. But eventually, you kids were born, and over the years, things got better for us financially and we got to travel and buy a house. Your father and I were able to get your grandma and *tías* green cards and I started to feel like it would all work out. Like I could really make a home for us in the states. Now, well now, I think I miss the idea of what the island used to be. *Lo que era.* But I know I could never live here again. My home is in America, with you, with the rest of the family. *Con la familia.*" In that moment, what she said had surprised even her and she choked up.

"But you still have family here too," I said, trying to comfort her.

"*Sí, pero* it's not the same." She laughed uneasily to break the tension and we both took a drink.

"Well," I said, "the island still is beautiful. And the people are so *alegre*, just singing and dancing all the time no matter what."

"*¿Y qué tú esperas?* What do you want them to do? Cry about their lives every day? It is what it is *mija* and they're just trying to make the best of it." And I knew that's all any of us was really trying to do in America or in the DR. Everyone had their cross to bear, it just came in different sizes, shapes, and colors of pain and grief. Our time at the resort helped us bond as a family and we were able to enjoy the "best" of what the island had to offer. We felt refreshed and rejuvenated, and ready to pursue our lives back in America.

The five of us left the island changed. For better or worse, we either felt a reconnect or a disconnect with a part of ourselves that only we understood. Whether it was my brother appreciating his *Taíno* ancestry or my father feeling proud of having left his legacy at the university, this was one family trip we would not easily forget. It was more than a trip; it was a journey that had been many years in the making. A journey where the road was made of sacrifices, hope, love and understanding.

My family has been forced to live like an island with no political party, president, or official language. We are not of any "new world" Columbus discovered. We are not Dominican enough or American enough to call either place home. We live and love with one foot on the ground and one foot in the sea. Yet, between these two worlds exists a place within each of us where we thrive, survive, and find the strength to pursue our own dreams. Dreams that allow us to never forget where we came from, so we can get to where we need to be, together as a family.

CPSIA information can be obtained
at www.ICGtesting.com
Printed in the USA
LVHW031704170121
676728LV00004B/817